LOVE AND
—OTHER—
BLESSINGS

This collection of poems is a true blessing. I found myself gently sighing warm affirmation, time and again, as I finished poem after poem. The poems warm the soul, quietly provoking and gently prodding towards a more grateful and grace-filled life.

Hamish Galloway
Moderator
Presbyterian Church of Aotearoa NZ

Glynn Cardy's blessings are sacred midwives of the ordinary, 'flowing, moving, cooling, offering life to all'. Rooted in the tradition of the Christian mystics, the reflections both comfort and challenge.

Originally written as oral presentations in a group setting, for me they are ideal for reading and experiencing while sitting under a tree, being nourished by the shade and protection – even the love – of nature. They are not to be gulped down in one session but individually savoured, coupled with a moment of contemplative, yea even prophetic, response. Highly commended.

Rex A E Hunt
Author, Progressive Liturgist, Religious Naturalist
Founding Director
The Centre for Progressive Religious Thought
Canberra

The rhythm of each blessing is very steady and soothing. I was always met with familiar feelings and similar settings.

Nestled within the blessings are many things that resonate with me. As a new grandmother, 'Bless this Child' is spot on. It hits a chord and makes a tune in my heart. It echoes the desires of my heart for my granddaughter. Thank you for putting into words what we who are too close often cannot express other than with 'ooohs' and 'ahhhs'.

I will definitely be dipping back into these fervent blessings with great abandon and great ease.

Rev. Alofa Lale
Mission Coordinator
Mercy Hospital, Dunedin
Associate Minister at First Church of Otago

LOVE AND OTHER BLESSINGS

GLYNN CARDY

Published in Australia by
Coventry Press
33 Scoresby Road
Bayswater VIC 3153

ISBN 9781922589279

Copyright © Glynn Cardy 2023

All rights reserved. Other than for the purposes and subject to the conditions prescribed under the *Copyright Act*, no part of this publication may be reproduced, stored in a retrieval system, or transmitted in any form or by any means, electronic, mechanical, photocopying, recording or otherwise, without the prior permission of the publisher.

Catalogue-in-Publication entry is available from the National Library of Australia
http://catalogue.nla.gov.au

Cover design by Ian James – www.jgd.com.au
Text design by Coventry Press
Cover photograph by Steve Bradley
Typeset in Tex Gyre Pagella

Printed in Australia

Contents

Introduction		8
1	Blessed is love	11
2	Bless all who try	12
3	Bless the busted nail	14
4	May we be blessed with eyes of the heart	15
5	Bless this child	16
6	Bless this place called home	17
7	Blessed are injuries	18
8	Blessed are moments found	20
9	Blessed are our cats	21
10	Blessed are the teaspoons	22
11	Blessed are we the forgiving	23
12	Blessed are the days of waiting	24
13	May you be blessed with enough wisdom	25
14	Blessed are those brief moments of gift	26
15	Blessed be those who mourn	27
16	Faith is a river	28
17	An Easter blessing	29
18	May you be blessed with little things	30
19	Blessed are those who can open	31
20	Blessed are those who cling to hope	32
21	To the end	33
22	Blessed are those who include	34
23	Blessed be the unpleasant stuff	36
24	Blessed are those who see in a child's offering	37
25	Blessed are those who seek the common good	38
26	Blessed are those who sit where they aren't supposed to	39
27	Blessed are we with eyes to see	40
28	Blessed are you who know the joy	41
29	Blessed be flowers	42
30	Blessed be hot-water bottles	43

31	Blessed be loving	44
32	A non-binary blessing	45
33	Blessed be Spring	46
34	Blessed be that evening walk	47
35	Blessed be the clown	48
36	Blessed be the lemon tree	49
37	Blessed be the moment	50
38	Blessed be the single thread	51
39	Blessed be the small shop in a small-town street	52
40	Blessed be the threads of love	53
41	Bless this place	54
42	Blessed be those who gather	55
43	Faithfully subversive	56
44	Blessed be your birthday	57
45	Blessed be those who are losing the ability to worry	58
46	Blessed encouragements	59
47	Blessed is a bouncy dog	60
48	May you be visited by hope	61
49	Blessed is a world where all races share	62
50	Blessed is an aroma of hope	63
51	Blessed is friendship	64
52	Blessed is cake to share	66
53	A nutty blessing	67
54	A wedding blessing	68
55	Blest with Summer Sun	70
56	Blessed is this home of straw	71
57	Blessed laughter	72
58	Blessed morning	73
59	Blessed relief	74
60	On towards the next bend	76
61	Hope is a fickle thing	77
62	Last Rites	78
63	Christmas blessing	79
64	Blessed be the melancholy	80
65	May a bundle of paradox bless you	82

66	New Year blessings	83
67	May we be blessed by the song of the deep bush	84
68	May the sun shine within you	85
69	May we be blessed by a river	86
70	May our days be filled with kindness	87

Introduction

A blessing is a way of finding and being found by grace.

On the one hand, a blessing begins with noticing the great and small, the serendipitous and the surprising, indeed all things that come into our lives. A blessing invites us to notice, appreciate, and be grateful. In so doing, not only are we blessed, but we bless others.

On the other hand, a blessing is something that arrives unbidden, coming when we least expect it, peeping around the corner of our consciousness, and inviting us to pause and take notice. It comes to comfort, to disturb, to strengthen, and to open the eyes of hearts.

Some of those things we notice are beautiful and uplifting, but others aren't. Hardship, heartache, and sometimes evil come our way, often due to no or little fault of our own. In the midst of these times, this noticing can offer us solace. And in the aftermath of such times, we can see things we've never really appreciated before.

Like our life itself. Like the love we have experienced. Like the fabulousness and frailty of flowers. Like the inquisitiveness of a child. Like the glorious smell of food. Like the gentle touch of a friend. Like coming home to ourselves and finding peace where we didn't think it could be.

Blessing has a religious pedigree and forms part of the Judaeo-Christian heritage, which in part has formed me. I grew up thinking a blessing was something ministers gave, on behalf of God, at the end of a church service. These blessings were theological statements about God, and what was imparted was this God's 'peace' and 'grace'.

Like my Celtic ancestors, and more modern Celtic writers, nowadays I prefer to imagine and articulate divinity woven into our lives, living, and environment. Like divine presence is in the road that rises to meet us, or in the deep peace of the running wave. 'Peace' and 'grace' are discovered, recovered, in our doing and being.

I don't often use the word G-o-d in blessings because it comes preloaded with metaphorical assumptions, usually patriarchal and monarchical. When I do use the word, I might put the 'g' in the lower case in order to signal the limits of our comprehension and the damage the uppercase understanding has often done.

Three of the themes that flow through these blessings are 'journey', 'love', and 'hope'. I think for those of us who have lived many decades and look back to see the patterns of our living – good memories and bad – we can appreciate that our life has been a journey with much richness along the route.

One such richness is love, in its many manifestations, and in the knowing that love has shaped us into who we are. Love of our family of origin, love of our family now, love of our friends and animals, love of acquaintances and strangers, love that communities can offer. To give, or be found by, the blessing of love is the greatest gift.

Hope is always a bit of mystery. Is it a by-product of love? Is it something we only know when life takes a turn for the worse? How do we give hope to others? How do we, when all seems lost, find hope? Or are we found by hope? Note, in saying 'found by' I'm not trying to divinise hope or love, rather simply point out that they can be beyond our reason and control.

You will find that I not infrequently use the words 'heart' and 'soul'. These words have no precise meaning, and I use them precisely because of that. They are pointers to feelings, to our intuitive sense that not all can be explained, and to our desire that we and the world be thought of and understood in more ways than the material, logical and reducible.

So, enjoy these blessings. They don't have to be read in any order. Dip into them. Play with them. Please feel free to use them and adapt them for your purposes (bearing in mind that if in a printed form then an acknowledgment is necessary).

Lastly, I would like to acknowledge and thank a few people who have assisted me in bringing this book of blessings to birth. To Hugh, my editor at Coventry, and to my friends Rob, Alexa and Rebecca, who have offered sage and welcome advice. Thank you for your humour, tolerance and ability to follow the meanderings of my imagination. To the photographers Steve, Simon, Sue, Masha and Kelvin, thank you for your eyes and skills in capturing beauty and your willingness to share. To the community of St Luke's

Presbyterian Church in Remuera, thank you for the generous license you give your clergy to create and to cross boundaries of convention.

For some forty years, I've had a companion on this journey of love and hope, my wife Stephanie. Together we have parented four wonderful children – Michael, Andrew, Maria and Anna – all of whom have shaped and made me into who I am. We have also had the care and delight of a number of animals, now just three – Cleo and Tigger (cats), and Finn (a Red Golden Retriever, see 'Blessed is a bouncy dog').

Stephanie has been beside me through the worst and in the best. She has informed and reformed my understandings about many things. But her greatest influence is in that which is really beyond understanding – matters of the heart and soul – a consequence of which is the eyes to see with gratitude the wonder, love and beauty of this life. This book is dedicated to her.

Glynn Cardy

Blessed is love

Blessed is a nurturing love,
warm-wrapped in daily affirmation,
knowing that whatever might happen,
there is someone who has you at heart,
ready to be what you need at hand,
ready beside imparting strength.

Blessed is a wild love,
that comes upon you like a gust of wind,
whipping your hair, filling you with possibility,
propelling you forward, lifting the heart.
It will not leave you the same.
Once felt never forgotten.

Blessed is the love of a dog,
snuggling in to that empty space,
touching you with need and affection,
ready to be, do, eat, go, and explore
with kinaesthetic pleasure,
a constant in rhythm with the heart.

Blessed is a well-aged love,
having travelled many a road,
having rounded many a bend,
having known much happiness,
cares were assuaged, the stars smiled,
and home was together.

Bless all who try

Bless all who try,
who speak up, out, often,
who stand, protest, and decry
the strong preying on the weak,
while the weak pray for relief,
and relief is hard
to find.

Bless all who give,
who get up, get out, get help,
threading, remaking, mending lives,
patching the ripped, sewing
the tears of the weary,
knitting a whole,
with care.

Bless all who fail,
who reach out and get rejected,
who stand up to be counted,
when no one is counting,
no one is watching,
no one cares.
Not here.

Bless all who try again,
who rise again, stand again,
who say 'Injustice, you're wrong!'
who say to each other 'Keep strong!'
who sing songs of wild hope,
and make them real,
again.

Bless all who try, fail, try again,
baring their truth to half-truths,
carrying carefully a dream that
one day the world will know itself
as together one garment
each stitch dependent,
cherished.

Bless the busted nail

Bless the busted nail,
yours, mine, it.
Bless the tiny incidentals,
yours, mine, them.
Bless the insignificant bits.

Blessed are we when
busted, tiny, insignificant.
Blessed are we who care about others
busted, tiny, insignificant,
and value, learn from, and honour them.

May the busted teach us strength.
May the tiny teach us tenacity.
May the insignificant teach us humility.

This is the wisdom of the wee,
a speck in the eye that gifts
a vision that notices thee.

May we be blessed with eyes of the heart

May we be blessed with eyes of the heart,
mystical seeing, what love gives,
that seventh sense, that bearer of hope,
the friend who waits for us when we're slow.

May we be blessed with eyes of the heart,
to know that deeply and truly we are surrounded,
held and upheld by the many hands and generosity
of those who believe in us, and always will.

May we be blessed with eyes of the heart,
to see what can be seen through a glass darkly,
to hear what can be heard when whispered by grace,
to know what can be known beyond all reason.

It is a beautiful thing to see with, and be seen by,
the eyes of the heart.

Bless this child

Bless this child,
born to be kind,
born to be wild,
like the wind,
inspirited.

May this child's
dreams come to pass,
and if they don't,
may new dreams arise.

For it is in listening
that we learn to listen;
it is in letting go,
that we learn to let go,
and it is in being loved,
that we learn to love.

Bless this child
born to play,
born to smile,
so peace may
come.

May the wisdom of old
shelter and warm you;
may the bonds of friendship
guide and encourage you,
and may love's whisper
call you to great things,
when you are ready.

Bless this place called home

Bless this place, that face,
at hearth warming our soul,
by the firelight known,
by the friendship given,
even in our fragility,
that look called home.

Bless this space, this grace,
secure, maybe, probably,
here our fears calmed,
here gentleness is balm,
here food is shared by
that look called home.

Bless this happiness held,
of knowing protection,
of knowing belonging,
of knowing a friend who
cares deeply enough to
be one called home.

Blessed are injuries

Blessed are injuries
we carry wearily,
reminders of age,
of fragility,
and mortality,
sites of resistance,
of pretence that
youth has not left us.

Blessed are injuries
where we tried, failed,
thought we could
when we couldn't,
thought we might
when in motion,
stepped, slipped,
and fell. Again.

Blessed are injuries,
memories of adventures,
sites of failure,
memorials to trying,
places of pain,
experience bodily etched,
bones with mended cracks,
a route to empathy.

Blessed are injuries
that lead us to enlarge
the boundaries of our hearts,
to include all who suffer,
whether by their doing or others,
and embrace and hold them,
so their pain is merged,
and somehow lessened.

Suffering, though never sought,
offers us a wisdom taught.

8

Blessed are moments found

Blessed are moments found
where worry and weariness
fade from the foreground,
and a mist-like calm settles,
and we are at rest.

Blessed are we who lie
under the yellowing Ginkgo*
that hard weight gone this day,
free now to pray and think, so
free to be restored.

Blessed are those who are
midwives of moments such,
bringers of gifts – food and care,
harbingers of hope, of much
balm for the soul.

Blessed are the moments
without the anxious thoughts,
pressing demands, omens
of dread, when we are naught
but a safe child again.

* *Ginkgo biloba, commonly known as ginkgo, is a species of tree native to China.*

Blessed are our cats

Blessed are our cats
with simple needs:
ample food with pats,
warm lap while we read.

Blessed are the content,
not seeking gain or reward,
quiet, relaxed, by intent,
the heart's eye restored.

Blessed is that inner eye
seeing the folly of more,
an insatiable drive that ties,
always keeping score.

Blessed are our furry friends
that show us the way home,
to that quiet place, the end,
waiting while we roam.

Blessed are the teaspoons

Blessed are the teaspoons,
little stirrers,
dainty dispensers,
designed for those who like
the elegant small.

Blessed are the tiny useful,
often unnoticed
until missing.
Potato peelers, nail scissors.
The practical small.

Blessed are those wee words
that tumble a sentence
so its oddity sticks,
and our heart might notice
this small grace.

Not all that is big, or bigger,
or designed to be desired,
meets our need.
Sometimes it's something
small.

Blessed are we the forgiving

Blessed are we the forgiving:
who didn't stoop to shun or shame
the ones who'd hurt us or threatened,
and kept the door ajar
in case.

Blessed are we the fallen:
who tripped and fell and failed,
or were pushed by need or greed,
and then found a door
still open.

Blessed are we the fragile:
wrapped up tight, secure, walled,
keeping hurt and blame at bay,
yet seeking a doorway
to trust.

Blessed is forgiveness and we so lucky
to know it, walk it, share it.

Blessed are the days of waiting

Blessed are the melancholy days,
when life is stilled, awaiting
for a shift, lift to the cold haze,
our hope in need of awakening.

Blessed are the fearful days,
when all happiness seems lost,
we wrap memories round and pray
for resilience to weather this frost.

Blessed are the cooler days,
when the air is crisp and bracing,
unseen sprouts ready to rise,
with our winter finally abating.

Blessed are the days of waiting,
of not seeing but hoping that a Spring
of good things will come and stay again,
warm hearts and friendship bringing.

May you be blessed with enough wisdom

May you be blessed with enough wisdom
to know what you don't know,
to trust what you do,
and to act on it.

May you be blessed with enough stupidity
to risk doing what can't be done,
to try anyway and fail,
and not lose hope.

May you be blessed with enough love,
flowing to and from you,
to strengthen and sustain
your fragile heart.

May you be found and lost and found again,
on this jumbled joyous journey,
guided by the light of paradox
into god.

And may you find friends on the path,
and be a friend to others,
and yourself.

Blessed are those brief moments of gift

Blessed are those brief moments of gift,
when the serendipitous slips into the sacred,
when a lucky coincidence becomes
a strange warming of the heart.

Blessed is the hand there to be held and
the one holding, both on to the life that flows,
in, through, under the expected, hoping...
as the beeping monitors serenade.

Blessed is the untimed arrival of a friend,
sitting, watching, serene, presence as prayer,
wordlessly knitting a sacred garment
of moments past with moments present.

Blessed is that bird on the outside sill,
visiting each day, as if to say, 'Are you okay?'
No wonder holy spirits are oft ornithic,
leaving a gift, a crevice in time.

Blessed are those brief moments of gift,
when the serendipitous slips into the sacred,
when a lucky coincidence becomes
a strange warming of the heart.

Blessed be those who mourn

Blessed be those who mourn
who enter the nothingness,
who remember slowly,
who, in time, turn their hands,
ready to touch and be touched, again.

Blessed are the dead who go
and yet remain, lingering,
tending our memories,
as we turn to the hurting
who await our ears, hands, and passion.

Blessed are those who rage
against all that sucks out joy
– those destructive deeds
and indifference;
for anger can seed and water
strength, resilience.

Blessed are those who give birth
to beautiful blossoms of hope:
kind words, smiles, quiet chuckles,
a place where all wounds are tended,
and justice and joy lovingly embrace.

Faith is a river

Blessed are those for whom
faith is a river,
winding its way through the
gullies and valleys of living,
irrigating land and crops,
quenching thirst...
to play in, to fish in.

And the river changes
in volume, in mood,
in clarity, in purpose.
And we change too.

Blessed are those for whom
God also changes.
The God of our past floats away,
or just dissolves into irrelevancy,
and we discover another
different divinity,
where we dissolve into
the oneness of all love,
compassion.

An Easter blessing

May we know the dawn light
arising from the gloom,
gracing the hilltops.

May we know the beauty of bird song
arising from the quiet,
delighting our hearts.

May we know the acceptance of others
arising from our times together
sharing food and stories.

May we know life arising.
May we know hope arising.
May we know love arising,
casting out all fear,
and welcoming in joy.

And may we be thankful for all these signs of god walking among us.

May you be blessed with little things

May you be blessed with little things:
a shy smile, a door held open,
a driver forgiving your infraction,
a cat who chooses your lap,
a young child's wet kiss,
the gift of unearned trust.

May you be blessed with offerings:
a hot brew on a blurry morning,
birds feeding out the window,
the ability to slow eat savouring,
to be in the moment,
to let worries go unheeded.

May you be blessed with heartstrings:
in tune with age, pulled tender,
to weep with your and others' loss,
to embrace happenstance,
to find touch and laugh a lot,
to face the day with brave content.

May you be blessed with little things.

Blessed are those who can open

Blessed are those who can open
their doors, tables, and hearts,
letting the known and unknown
come in.

Blessed are those who absorb
others' quirks, hurts, and foibles,
with good humour and calm,
gracefully.

Blessed are those hosts who know
that they are in turn welcomed and
needed, as they welcome and
feed others.

Blessed are those hosted who know
and appreciate the vulnerability that such
welcome might bring. Respect going
both ways.

Blessed are we when we open,
absorb, welcome, need, feed, appreciate,
and allow others to gently return
the same.

Blessed are those who cling to hope

Blessed are those who cling to hope,
even, especially, when all is bleak,
and the tide of good memories
has ebbed and gone.

Blessed are the silent strollers,
who along the shoreline seek
belief in anything that will
soothe their aches.

Blessed are the shore creatures,
waving and squawking, disturbing
the loneliness of despair,
with their familiarity.

Blessed are those who offer not wealth,
know-what, or even wisdom,
but stroll beside, belief-giving,
leaking hope.

To the end

Blessed are those who don't call it a day,
who don't walk away, or surrend,
those staying to help the helpless,
may they endure to the end.

Blessed are those who find passion,
purpose, fulfilment, and friends,
in giving out, away, compassion,
staying loyal to the end.

Blessed are you who alone stand,
when others have left or descend
into tranquil warm normality
and you, bracing, face the end.

May you know when all is said and seemingly lost,
the peace of loving when all seemingly was in vain,
the peace of giving when all seemingly was to gain,
the peace of losing when all seemingly was to win,
the peace of choosing when all actually has been
to the end a wonderful blessed cost.

Blessed are those who include

Blessed are
those who include,
and those asking to be,
pushing our boundaries,
inviting us to enlarge
our minds and our hearts
so all might belong.

Blessed is
the long-rutted road,
from a path of privileges,
to a forest of pathways,
from what was to will be,
walking from security
to uncertainty.

Blessed will be
the little encouragements:
shared scroggin*, a song,
smiles, a night shelter,
and friendships that
endure beyond
the bounds of time.

Blessed as it happened,
a fork came
one path clear,
the other not,
one way with rewards.

Yet we were following a thread,
or so we hoped,
and clung on
to grace.

Blessed are
those who include,
and those asking to be,
paths crossing, hurts,
respect given, held.
It can be a long road,
this winding life.

* Scroggin, also known as trail mix, is a mixture of dried fruit, nuts, and other food that is a staple snack for most hikers.

Blessed be the unpleasant stuff

Blessed be the unpleasant stuff,
that resides without but seeps in,
embarrassingly, frequently,
like resentment, like anger,
like blaming, like shaming.

Blessed be this hurtful stuff,
that we've tried to hide away,
told it's wrong, bad, maybe sin,
it has festered away within,
needing light, air, to clear.

Blessed be the moment when
another's uplifting allows an airing,
the start of a clearing,
when the rocks are moved
to see, to free,
what's beneath.

Blessed be the delicate moment,
when what we long fear is seen,
our ugly, our hurt that has been,
is revealed, but not repelled,
a woundedness ripe for healing.

Blessed be those who take a risk,
bringing the unsightly unseen
to light, so that they might try
to receive some healing again,
rather than stay with the known,
familiar grumbles and regrets.

Blessed are those who see in a child's offering

Blessed are those who see
in a child's offering, the hope
that can meet our neighbours' needs,
and the need of our own hearts.

It is a small thing,
to share your lunch
in the playground,
or the office.

Blessed are those who see
in the caring and courtesy,
in the kindness and grace extended,
god being born, again.

It is a small thing,
to give birth to god –
letting generosity within
expand into generosity out.

Blessed are those who see
that all is a movement of giving,
receiving, grace, and surprise,
able to sustain and feed the world.

Blessed are those who seek the common good

Blessed are those who seek the common good
even when it's not their own,
caring for those who don't care for them,
caring for those who can't or won't be good.

Blessed are those who've learnt and give empathy
without needing reciprocity,
without needing recognition or reward.
They emanate contentment – like angels.

Blessed are those tireless encouragers,
who see the best in the worst,
who see the light in the cracks of our lives,
who lead us, guide us, bring us home to our heart.

26

Blessed are those who sit
where they aren't supposed to

Blessed are those who sit
where they aren't supposed to,
who are quietly disruptive,
of place and its peace.

Blessed are those who knowing
their place sit elsewhere,
wander around, itinerant,
disturbers of right order.

Blessed are those out of order,
playing with their food and politics,
who laugh at seriousness,
upsetters of laid plans.

Blessed are we when room is made
for the ordered and disordered,
for the settlers and disturbers,
for a big table, broad enough for all.

Blessed are we with eyes to see

Blessed are we with eyes to see,
in our simple offering, the hope
that can meet our neighbours' needs,
and the need of our own hearts.

Blessed are we with eyes to see,
in grace given and in kindnesses,
in the caring and the courtesy,
god sprouting, again and again.

Blessed are we with eyes to see,
there is no divide betwixt divinity and me,
for swirls of grace hold, give, receive,
all life in a movement of gift.

Blessed are we with eyes to see,
together, that movement, are we.

Blessed are you who know the joy

Blessed are you who know the joy
of trusting another with your past,
to be there whatever the future,
and to hold and embolden you now.

Blessed are you who know contentment,
morning grace and evening rest,
kind words, gentle touch, music of giving –
an all-pervading harmony.

Blessed are you who know the love
which champions you, cries with you,
and catches you when you crash –
a love that endures to the end.

Blessed are you who know the serenity
of sitting in companionable silence,
listening to the unspoken, hearing
the beat of memory and promise.

Blessed be flowers

Blessed be flowers
enticing our senses,
brightening our days,
delighting our hearts.

Blessed be flowers
footprints of fairies,
the dance of this day,
ephemeral and fabulous.

Blessed be flowers
beauty reaching our need,
bounty touching our frailty,
budding wildly to lift us.

Blessed be flowers
given to comfort,
given to celebrate,
love's sensual cloak.

Blessed be flowers
colouring our lives with joy,
scenting them out richly,
to blossom the world.

Blessed be hot-water bottles

Blessed be hot-water bottles,
warm comfort in a cold bed,
or on a lap when the air is cold,
or against an aching back.
Little can make a difference.

Blessed be hot-water bottles,
simple in design and application,
practical and unregulated,
soothing us, inducing rest.
Comfort can be uncomplicated.

Blessed are those who emulate
the ways of the hot-water bottle,
giving warmth and comfort,
to sleepers and sufferers.
We can be bearers of relief.

The prayer of the hot-water bottle:
'May our bodies at rest find the calm
we need to steer our hearts from harm,
in sleep to flourish and in hope awake
our nightly renewal a balm does make.'

Blessed be loving

Blessed be loving,
simple, sometimes, most,
when a wee word warms.

Blessed be loving,
complex, times some,
when our feelings are at odds,
awaiting even.

Blessed be waiting,
simple, patient time,
when getting ready takes long.

Blessed be waiting,
complex, holding time,
when a beloved is dying short.
We aren't ready.

Blessed be tears,
simple, glad drips,
when laughing silly, loudly, often.

Blessed be tears,
complex, sad, dripping,
when unexpectedly a kind word
touches our soul.

Loving, waiting, tearing,
these rhythms are blest,
profoundly simple and complex.

A non-binary blessing

May we be blessed with eyes
of the soul to see beyond
the binary categories
of right and wrong,
of winners and losers,
male and female.

May we be blessed with eyes
to imagine lots of room,
space for us too in our guise,
whatever our nom de plume,
a place for strange, different,
and the despairing.

May we be blessed with eyes
of others to see the whole,
the unity of difference,
the delight of the soul,
the play of shadows,
a nest for sojourners.

A non-binary world is indeed a blessing,
the habitat of angels.

Blessed be Spring

Blessed be Spring springing,
flowering colours, baby lambs,
new life and vibrancy bringing,
goddess of starting again.

Blessed be Spring springing,
days stretching, warmth returning.
We revel in the signs of Summer:
Winter has been turned.

From cold to warm,
from dark to light,
from absence to joy,
from barren to bright,
born again.

Blessed be Spring springing,
a turning of our eyes, our mood,
from sleeping to start, beginning
to unfurl, with gratitude.

(*Photo: Simon Salomé-Bentley*)

Blessed be that evening walk

Blessed be that evening walk,
along the paths we well know,
hearing the quieting sounds,
of a day drawing to a close.

Blessed time when work is done,
and thoughts now freed to roam,
over life's currents and eddies,
finding driftwood to bring home.

Blessed be our companions,
sentinels on our nightly stroll,
voices of joy, love, and hope,
stilling our disquieted soul.

Blessed be twilight compline,
gentle repose of the day.

(Photo: Kelvin Wright)

Blessed be the clown

In 1981, the rugby team representing the racist apartheid regime in South Africa toured in New Zealand. Thousands took to the streets to protest. In one of the infamous acts of that time, protesting clowns were beaten. The former New Zealand Times *journalist Pekka Paavonpera described what he saw: 'As the clowns were cowering, the three police officers began hitting them with their riot sticks, prodding them in the stomach. They kept going 'til all three had slumped to the ground'.*

Blessed be the clown,
the jokester, prankster, fool,
bringing the house down
with levity, seriously, who'll
now wear the sore cost of it.

Hold up a mirror to power,
laugh at its righteous face,
be unflinching as its glowers,
for its angry violence braced...
they bore the raw cost of it.

Blessed be the clowns,
disturbers of the concrete
of certainty and truth owned
by those controlling speech.
They air the awful cost of it.

To laugh at yourself in a clown,
to give the weak outsider voice,
to upend, turn things upside-down,
to jest rules, offer another choice,
clowns wore the fear cost of it.

Blessed be the lemon tree

Blessed be the lemon tree,
fecund shapely yellows,
scenting with bounty,
lifting our gloomy weary,
ever-cheery.

Blessed be the lemon drink,
staying winter's snuffles,
stirred with honey, water,
served with care, calm,
soothing balm.

Blessed be gift of lemon,
antimicrobial cleanser,
perfuming house, garden,
there for drinks, baking,
happy making.

Blessed be taste of lemon,
icing, limoncello, cakes,
pies, puddings, pancakes,
ceviche, candied peel,
tangy taste feel.

Blessed be the lemon tree,
alone in the backyard,
not for climbing, huts,
shade, picnics, but
for loving life.

Blessed be the lemon tree.

Blessed be the moment

Blessed be the moment,
when time so early late,
its relevance not reset,
caused the rockfall of fate
to cease to be a threat.
A timeless moment.

Blessed be that moment,
of not caring about worry,
of what others might think,
of who we are or will be,
when into stillness we sink.
A timeless moment.

Blessed be this moment,
when all is well regardless,
loss and its treasures fade,
all manner well regardless,
here where peace is plaid.
A timeless moment.

Blessed be the moment,
never and always yet here,
graceful hope flowering there,
place of ease, welcome, care,
space for wonder and prayer.
A timeless moment.

Blessed be such moments.

Blessed be the single thread

Blessed be the single thread,
broken off, left to fray underfoot,
not noticed, not picked up, unseen
by the traffic of privileged progress.
Alone, silent, singular.

Blessed be the single word,
leaping from its context bound,
to lodge irritatingly in the gears
of our mind, disrupting the rhythm.
A quiet word of protest.

Blessed be the single stroke,
when a splash of beauty breaks
onto the bland canvas hanging,
difference making a difference,
to celebrate the different.

Blessed be the single track,
unpromising, less trod, overgrown,
taken only by fools and frisky dogs,
a place where prayers and other
useless things are thrown.

Grace weaves with a thread downtrod,
Grace whispers with a disturbing word.
Grace paints with a rebel brush wild.
Grace walks a nothing track to nowhere.
With such grace we are blessed.

Blessed be the small shop in a small-town street

Blessed be the small shop in a small-town street,
which provides the novelty of yesterday's pace,
a shop where you're known by name, a homely retreat.
This is a welcoming space, not in the race
for more growth, gain, or fashionable greed,
but content to be the size of our need.

Blessed be the unrealistic small-timers, the time-less,
who abscond from the ideology of bustle and hustle,
defining success as expansion and profit, mindless
'bigger-is-better' myths, and the struggle and tussle
of getting there, from the weary climb to nowhere,
from 'please-give-me-give-me-more' the only care.

Blessed be those who haven't kept up, who walk slow,
smiling at the day, listening without ear phones,
stopping to greet a friend or stranger to say hello,
noticing the gentle things, the small unknowns,
and grateful that the highway to busyness
has bypassed this place of happiness.

Blessed be the threads of love

Once when I was very sick, clinging to life,
I had a dream that I was far up in the night sky,
nothing above, beneath, beside, or behind,
except silver threads coming out of the darkness,
connecting to me and holding me suspended.
Each thread was an incandescent filament of love,
reaching in, holding, and sustaining me.

Blessed be the threads of love,
that hold us in our darkest times,
sustaining us by being there,
though we know not how.

Blessed be the threads of love,
each one as weak as kindliness,
and as strong as slivers of light,
stabilising us as our world spins.

Blessed be the threads of love,
whisperings, prayer, letters,
sealed strong, mailed from the heart,
arriving par avion in ours.

Blessed be the threads of love,
light in our darkness, silent joy,
sustaining the soul, holding us tight,
as hope draws her next breath.

Bless this place

Blessed be this place
where it is safe to be
awake to all possibility.

Bless this sacred space,
centre of our gathering,
our talk, silence, prayer.

Blessed be the bread broken:
symbol, sustenance, gift…
what we are and more.

Bless this song sung
that calls to our souls:
to let go, be open, giving.

Blessed be our together body:
fragile, strong, expectant,
a colourful tapestry becoming.

Bless this place
safe to be
awake to all.

Blessed be those who gather

Blessed be those who gather
to sit, to talk, to share,
to be together weaving
strands of life, of care,
into one single soul moment.

Blessed be those who gather
in spite of all that shatters,
that apart pulls, corrupts
good and generous matters,
with the curse of distrust.

Blessed are those who gather
for respite and to ignite
the bonds of friendship
that can sustain and unite
along the lonesome beat.

Blessed are we gathered,
laughing with room for more,
in this soul-enriching space,
big tables, hope, food galore,
hear the mercy of grace.

Faithfully subversive

Blessed be those who don't know their place,
who get up when told to sit down there,
who speak up when told to their face,
you're not welcome, needed round here.
May they be faithfully obstinate.

Blessed be those who push back, resist,
for whom a 'no' is a pause, a comma,
who stand into the rain and icy hiss,
and don't submit to a rage that's gonna
blow rough if you don't acquiesce.

Blessed be subversives, erring wild,
painting swiggles outside lines they stray,
seeing hope in a child's unfettered play,
seeing folly in seeking big time pay,
and lamenting our obsequience.

Blessed that faithful rebellious lead,
taking us beyond our sureties,
our vision not bound by what we see,
our wisdom not bound by what we need,
our love not bound by self-serving creeds.

Blessed be your birthday

Blessed be your birthday,
family and friends offer cheer,
cake, candles, gifts, a bouquet,
fondness felt, even a shed tear.

Blessed be your birthday,
coming ready or not every year,
age on the increase needless to say,
time to consider what we hold dear.

Blessed be your birthday,
dearest connections, love, bonds,
memories precious, hear to say,
inviting us all to respond.

Blessed be your birthday,
when we remember that you
are the gift we celebrate today,
wondrous, cherished, a friend true.

Blessed be those who are losing the ability to worry

Blessed be those who are losing the ability to worry,
who have met their fears and are slowly accepting them,
realising that life, love, and loss are all gifts intertwined,
fellow travellers, inseparable companions on their journey.
They are paddling with the river, rounding the bends.

Blessed be those with the wisdom to let moments unfold,
without planning, making, and guiding things to happen,
who have the courage to let life meet them and teach them,
rather than telling life when and what it can and can't do.
They are paddling with the river, rounding the bends.

Blessed be those who have no interest in controlling others,
and in the conflicts that ensue, consume, and destroy,
seeking instead to find the good in the other, even if hard,
for somewhere somehow way back we are all related.
They are paddling with the river, rounding the bends.

Blessed be those who let laughter come in, break smiles,
tell tall tales, and stay, a place set in their heart for friends
and friends-to-be, whoever passes their way, the worriers,
the weary, the wanting, all who need the good food of grace.
They are paddling with the river, rounding the bends.

Blessed be those who are learning to expect nothing, happily,
to judge not, even when they are judged, to judge not their self,
giving thanks for each moment met, each wee morsel received,
enjoying what is and will be, without wanting any more or less.
They are paddling with the river, rounding the bends.

Blessed encouragements

Blessed encouragements –
a warm smile, touch sensing need,
a walking song heard in the trees,
a welcome shelter with fire kind,
a wacky story to ease the mind –
come 'compass us round.

Blessed encouragements –
friendships woven lengthy, tight,
food shared heartening the night,
fabulous whānau*, mixed we meld,
fatigued I stumbled but was held –
come 'compass us round.

Blessed encouragements –
a small child who gifts us a trusting long,
a saga where the weak are s'prisingly strong,
a support given when feeling dismayed,
a strength gifted with empathy conveyed –
come 'compass us round.

Encouragement is a blessing
missed most when missing.

A Māori word for extended family, or family grouping.

Blessed is a bouncy dog

Blessed is a bouncy dog,
who revels in rollicking,
a bounding appetite
for unabashed joy,
regardless of
the rain.

The rain of misery falls,
in this gloomy season,
driving away the good,
beautiful, hopeful,
with a wash
of criticism.

Blessed is a monarch butterfly,
brightening colours proud,
upon a drab slab wet wall,
a sparkle of difference,
an advent of beauty,
a protest.

The dog runs, flips over, and
slides, muddy, and wet.
The gloom of our sky,
worries, and news,
can't dampen his
inspirited heart.

(Photo: Sue Dick)

May you be visited by hope

May you be visited by hope,
and may she stay awhile.

May the song she sings
give your tired face a smile,
ease what worries bring,
and let fears rest a while.
May her music reverberate
in all those dark and lonely
corridors where you spend
too long.

May she come like a gale,
blowing in from the sea,
biting cold, piercing hail,
proclaiming you're alive,
ready for more, not less.
May she steady your fears,
ready your mind, steel
your heart.

May you accept her gift,
of comforting melody,
of whistling wind lifting,
moving aside what is,
to allow what might be,
to come and find a home
in that bedraggled debris,
this life.

May you be visited by hope,
and may she stay awhile.

Blessed is a world where all races share

Blessed is a world where all races share
what is valued, none are violated,
and the joys and beauty of life are accessible to all.

Blessed is a world where all people
are treated with dignity and respect,
and everyone has a safe place called home.

Blessed is a world where peace is the ground of justice,
justice is guided by compassion,
and compassion is gifted unconditionally.

Blessed is a world where we have the courage
and inspiration to build such a vision,
and the faith and trust in each other to sustain it.

Blessed is an aroma of hope

Blessed is an aroma of hope
that can come when
a smile and hospitality
expand into friendship,
or its possibility.

Blessed is hope's delight
that infuses us when
our lamp is burning low
and despair can loom,
unbidden.

Blessed is a refreshing wind
that blows gently, soothing
our worries and fears,
inviting us to feel the breath
of hope.

Blessed is hope that comes
through the front door or back,
stays awhile, puts the kettle on,
giving comfort that lingers
long after.

Blessed is friendship

Blessed is friendship,
sitting in satiated silence,
sipping the joyous serenity,
drawn into something more
than the two of us,
something hard to describe,
and just knowing,
knowing without why.

Blessed friendship
when struggle and suffering
arrive to enlarge their space,
suffocating promise and ease.
Friendship is there, in the storm,
finding words, offering touch,
keeping the fears at bay.

Blessed is friendship
when we venture into
the desolate dark unknowing
where death is felt,
where light flickers,
and our soul needs and
finds unexpected strength.

Blessed friendship,
there is much sorrow
when the mooring that bound
us is finally broken by death,

and a great floodtide of wanting
envelops our soul,
and sucks us out to sea.

Blessed is friendship
as we are guided by the horizon,
the dreams of justice and grace
peeking out from the clouds,
whispering encouragements,
as we point our prow out,
beyond the breakers of death.

Blessed is cake to share

Blessed is cake to share:
in the making,
licking the spoon,
in the baking,
inhaling the smell,
in the eating,
with guests satiated...
divine.

Blessed is communing,
being knit together,
to make and create,
to inspire and build,
to cooperate and care,
to laugh and help,
to heal the world...
divine.

Blessed are kitchens
catering for the spiritual,
and churches catering
for the appetite,
and we lucky enough
to find the divine
in both, and fold them
together.

A nutty blessing

Blessed is peanut butter,
as smooth as you like,
in satay, cakes, or raw,
spread, licked, or mixed,
with toast, butter, jam,
decorating our lips,
satisfying.

Blessed is peanut butter,
daily desirable delectable,
a taste of yesteryears,
when life was simpler,
here to stay, a staple
of our comfort pantry,
and table.

If we are what we eat
then mostly we are nuts,
crunchy tasty presents,
slathering some relief,
over rumpled-up spirits,
run over and down by
life's exigencies.

Blessed is peanut butter,
large jar passed around,
lid off, knife dug in, goodness
extracted and spread thick
over the bread of our living,
kinder communion,
a nutty hope.

A wedding blessing

Blessed is the gifting of love
that believes in you,
that finds joy in the we,
finds strengths in the common,
and dreams arising in the wings.

Blessed is the gifting of love
that believes in you,
which hears the voices minor,
encourages the trust major,
and sings the heart to soar.

Blessed is the gifting of love
that believes in you,
is gentle sloping always,
is hopeful facing always,
and is steadfastly stubborn, always.

Blessed is the gifting of love,
that believes in you,
is weak as well as strong,
is balm to calm, soothe,
the soul's homecoming.

Blessed is the gifting of your love,
it believes in you –
may you know its courage,
may you know its wisdom,
and may you know its beauty.

So, may the dawn chorus always sing for you,
the night melodies rest and regenerate you,
the trees wave at and encourage you,
the wind dance around and uplift you,
the playful sea surround and delight you;
and may you always be known by arohanui*,
encompassing, holding, and emboldening you,
now and forever.

* A Māori word for deep affection, much love.

(Photo: Masha Steyn)

Blest with Summer Sun

May we be blest with summer sun
that warms the sand, the sea, and our hearts.
The gloom of the winter damp and cold
is expunged by this redeeming sparkling light.

May we be blest with good books to read,
and good conversations about them,
and good walks to aid our pondering them,
and a good dog to bring us home.

May we blest with the gifts of a beach,
of food to share with friends and passersby,
of a garden declaring its vibrant beauty,
and the infusion of gratitude in our soul.

May we be blest with enough illumination
to see the good in the world and want to add to it,
and to see the despair in the world and know
that the light we kindle together can help.

May we be blest with epiphanic light:
light within and light without,
light to see the diverging of paths,
and light to know the path to follow.

Blessed is this home of straw

Blessed is this home of straw,
wind-blown, fragile.
It is where I fit in,
whatever the size,
with familiar smells,
and I'm locked not in or out.

Blessed is this home of sticks.
Here I'll always belong,
I'm sticking with it,
trusting fears are gone,
here I'm valued as unique,
I am strong, I am weak.

Blessed is this home of bricks,
piled, layered, braced,
where hope is kilned,
where heart is kneaded,
an aromatic sanctuary
that no wolf can blow down.

Blessed laughter

Blessed laughter,
tonic that tickles, teases,
spilling levity into the gloom,
disturbing us with giggles,
lightening the room.

Blessed laughter,
a wild hose shower,
in summer's heat,
body and soul soak,
festive relief.

Blessed laughter,
irregularly inconvenient,
irregularly irreverent,
tripping us with smiles,
when we shouldn't.

Blessed laughter,
holy, healthy, heretical,
destabiliser of our boring,
too-serious selves, come
to lampoon and save.

Blessed morning

Blessed morning,
a night with little sleep ends,
a sick child rests, at peace,
and we, sore-tired, ascend,
commitments to keep.

Blessed sunlight,
come to gladden, revive
weary worried bones,
to see with grateful eyes
this blessing of home.

Blessed dog, cats,
creatures all greet the day,
come for food, touch, chat,
to comfort, bond, and say,
'Peace' and all of that.

Blessed relief

Blessed relief,
stopping, resting,
time-paused beneath
this alpine waterfall,
glacier-fed, insistent,
purposeless 'thrall,
that water flowing,
washing our aching body,
our weariness going,
our soul refreshed.

Blessed relief,
when visited by comfort,
and caressed into sleep,
soothing the tiredness,
as the rushing river sweeps,
massaging our needed rest.
There is a song,
that the river knows,
and it takes us along,
over the boulders of our dreams.

Blessed river,
a chorus of life
in the upper valleys,
where its joy is rife,
taming our thirst,
tingling our flesh,

tumbling our dreams,
and on it flows as a needed guest,
down to the parched lands
and towns below.

On towards the next bend

Blessed the winding road,
away nowhere somewhere on,
away from sureties trusted,
away from pleasantries past,
we go meandering, muddied,
on towards the next bend.

Blessed the windswept road,
from what was to what will be,
from who was I to who will be,
from the presence of certainty,
to the presents of maybes,
on towards the next bend.

Blessed be the wrong road,
this way taken back at the fork,
this choice taken by weary feet,
this route unfamiliar yet the beat
of my heart guided, girded me
on towards the next bend.

Blessed be these roads we go,
what steers us who really knows?
What sustains us as we stride,
what sure friend will walk beside
all iffy unknowns as we wend,
on towards the next bend.

(*Photo: Steve Bradley*)

Hope is a fickle thing

Hope is a fickle thing,
receding like the tide,
when our spirits ebb, weep,
sinking in tidal mud deep,
firm ground gone.

Hope is a funny thing,
returning like the sun,
when night's gloom melts,
blessed relief known, felt,
coming to gladden.

Hope is a fairy thing,
magical, gifting, twinkling,
arriving unbidden,
yet lifting to brighten
all so touched.

Hope is a faith thing,
acts that take courage,
the lack of sense to defy
what is plainly before our eyes,
and risk doing differently.

Last Rites

May the angels guard and comfort you,
as your soul leaves the bosom of this life,
the arms of your family and friends,
journeying to the great unknown.

There may you know yourself to be held,
by the strong and resilient threads of love,
spun between you and those loving you,
threads that we might call God.

May you remember us, holding our smiles.
May you forgive us, letting go of our hurts.
May you bless us, recalling the good times.
May you travel light and with love.

And may you know yourself,
as we've known you,
to be blessed,
and a blessing to others.

Rest this day, and forever more, in our peace.

Christmas blessing

Live as gently as you can,
wherever you can,
whenever you can.
For this is the path of peace.

Let go as gracefully as you can,
wherever you can,
whenever you can.
For this is the path of truth.

Love as generously as you can,
wherever you can,
whenever you can.
For this is the path of hope.

And may the blessings
of peace, truth, and hope,
be with you, your kin, and all,
this Christmas.

Blessed be the melancholy

Blessed be the melancholy,
for they have been refined
in the fire.

Are we blessed
who live to see this day,
when the night has been so long,
when yesterday's loss was all consuming,
and ache upon ache
piled up?

Blessed be the mooring memories,
that can come unbidden in these times,
gems unexpectedly found,
in the debris of sorrow,
glimpses of a joy once
believed in.

Blessed be a gentle whisper,
when we are laid low,
a salve for our weeping souls,
a warm wrap of grace.
What is this voice we hear?
Maybe hope can come again.

The sun is now sinking, day is done,
gone from the seas, hills, lake, sky,
all is not well,
and rest is not gentle,
yet blessedness is not far from us,
even nigh.

O Death and Misery flee,
let us be.

Blessed be the melancholy,
for their hope has been refined,
in the fire of loss.

(*Photo: Steve Bradley*)

May a bundle of paradox bless you

May a bundle of paradox bless you,
adding confusion, uncertainty,
to your well-worn creeds,
and gentleness to your
thoughts and deeds.

May the bundle be tied with a strawberry yarn,
that easily and frighteningly unravels,
like your sound judgments,
when touched with need's
fragile face.

Blessed be paradox,
bane of the orthodox,
balm of the heterodox,
allure of a faith whose divinity can't
be named thus tamed.

Blessed be the 'doxies,
those misfits, the odd, peculiar,
who disturb our familiar,
stretching, upside-downing,
transforming it.

Blessed be those who hear,
who invite a different wisdom,
the repast of the suffering,
the grace of the excluded,
to change them, forever.

New Year blessings

May blessings shower upon you
in this year ahead,
and may you recognise them.

May you be less lonely and aching
as you experience the cup of kindness
offered by other lonely and aching people.

May you breathe more freely, less fearfully,
as the destructive behaviour of others
is swept away by a tide of goodwill.

May you laugh more often,
find puddles to splash in,
and sing every day some.

May you know the gentle god
who goes by the name of hospitality
and be buoyed by Her embrace.

May the trickle of love you know grow
to become a cascading stream of hope
irrigating the courage in your soul.

And may you stand in the waterfall
of these and other blessings and say:
'It's good to be alive'.

May we be blessed by the song of the deep bush

May we be blessed
by the song of the deep bush,
singing green, singing hope,
lifting our spirits,
if only we can hear.

May we be blessed
by the boughs of the forest,
overshadowing, protecting,
calming our souls
if only we let them.

May we be blessed
by the god who holds
the 'is' and the 'not yet',
the pain of rampant destruction,
and the hope of vulnerable seedlings.

So come, sit, listen, be…
in this nest of the woodlands,
opening ourselves to the mystery
of the way, pace, and prayer of trees,
and their blessing.

May the sun shine within you

May the sun shine within you,
radiating warmth and welcome.

May the wind carry you free,
ferrying all your worries away.

May the rain nourish your soul,
gently tending the seeds of hope.

May the mountains surround you,
sheltering and inspiring your heart.

May the forests cool and comfort you,
as you care for and appreciate them.

May the rivers run through your being,
sustaining, empowering, refreshing.

And may you be a blessing to others:
a warm spirit, a free song,
a gentle soul, a strong heart,
a tenderer, a sustainer.

May we be blessed by a river

May we be blessed by a river,
flowing, moving, cooling,
offering life to all it touches,
from high in the hills,
across the flat lands,
until it reaches the coast.

May we be blessed by the insight
that, like the river, a sacred spirit
is also flowing, cascading,
touching life, offering hope,
refreshing our dry places,
revitalising our parched souls.

Sometimes a big river will carry us,
as we float, or boat, on it.
Sometimes the river will hold fish,
and its banks will be adorned with anglers.
Sometimes the river is still,
silently reflecting the beauty about.

May we be blessed by a river
that gently heals and soothes,
that picks us up and carries us on,
a spirit confidently moving,
consistent in purpose,
constant in its hope.

May our days be filled with kindness

May our days be filled with kindness,
as the sun that lights the sky,
and may we always have the courage,
to spread our wings and fly.

May our days be filled with light,
light without and light within,
light to welcome, greet and meet,
and wisdom to find grace therein.

May the clarity of the light be known,
may the ancestors protect and abide,
may the goodness of the earth be sown,
may the bounty of the seas survive.

May the dawn light find us awake and still,
ready to scheme, dream and be connected,
may evening find us gracious and fulfilled,
ready for the night sheltered and protected.

May our soul calm us, console, and renew,
enlarged by the nurture and gifts of others,
may our soul reflect light and hope through
our bidding home, sisters and brothers.

www.ingramcontent.com/pod-product-compliance
Lightning Source LLC
Chambersburg PA
CBHW012007090526
44590CB00026B/3906